fraturtles

words and pictures by Keith Greenstein

For my twin brother, Steven,
who's nothing like me. Or anyone.

"I like being a twin!" Shelly said to her friends,

"We are special, my brother and I."

"You're no twin!" roared her friends with a thunderous laugh.

"Don't you know that all twins look alike?"

But my mom said I am, Shelly thought to herself,
Yet I have to admit that it's true.
I don't look a thing like my brother at all.
Wait, does that mean he's not a twin, too?!

"We've got to get home!" Shelly screamed to her "twin."
Though she wasn't so sure anymore.
"Are we both twins or what?!" Shelly yelled to her mom
As she burst through the house's front door.

"Who the heck is this dude I've been with all my life?!
'Cause my friends say that twins look the same.
If they're right and it's true and I'm not a twin, mom,
Then I'm gonna need you to explain!"

"Calm down, Shelly-Belly," said Shelly's mom back.
"You ARE a twin, just like your brother.
You both shared the same belly at the same time.
And that makes you twins," said her mother.

"But, we don't look alike!" Shelly snapped at her mom,
"My hair's *blonde* and my brother's is *red!*
My friends say that twins look exactly the same.
Are they all just not right in the head?"

"You're *fraternal."* said mom with a comforting smile.

But this only made Shelly confused.

"Fraturtle?" asked Shelly, "Did you make that up?

If you did, I'm not one bit amused."

"Fra-ter-nal," mom said, "You are fra-ter-nal twins.
They are twins who don't look like each other.
They can be short & tall. They can be big & small.
They can even be sister and brother."

"Fraturtle," thought Shelly as she scratched her shell.
Then she turned and she looked at her brother.
And slowly a smile stretched across her whole face,
"I like it!" she said to her mother.

"Fraturtle!" she shouted as she grabbed her twin.
And she hugged him until he turned blue.
He might have passed out if she hadn't let go
But she did, because that's what twins do.

"I like being a twin!" Shelly shouted out loud.
"We're unique, my fraturtle and I!
"So, we don't look alike but who *cares!*" Shelly yelled,
"Because I get a best friend for life."

Made in the USA
San Bernardino, CA
25 April 2018